I WILL
NOT
LEAVE
YOU
DESOLATE

I WILL
NOT
LEAVE
YOU
DESOLATE

Martha
Whitmore
Hickman

ABINGDON
PRESS

I Will Not Leave You Desolate:
Some Thoughts for Grieving Parents

Copyright © 1982 by Martha Whitmore Hickman
Previously printed under ISBN 0-8358-0443-7 by The Upper Room

This book is printed on recycled, acid-free paper.

ISBN 0-687-00289-3

Scripture quotations not otherwise identified are from the Revised Stan-dard Version of the Bible, copyrighted 1946, 1952 and © 1971 by the Divi-sion of Christian Education, National Council of the Churches of Christ in the United States of America, and are used by permission.

Scripture passages designed KJV are from the King James Version of the Bible.

The poem "How Many Nights" is from *Body Rags* by Galway Kinnell, Copyright © 1967 by Galway Kinnel. Reprinted by permission of Houghton Mifflin Co.

Cover design by John Boegel
Illustrations by John Robinson

94 95 96 97 98 99 00 01 02 03 04 — 10 9 8 7 6 5 4 3 2 1

MANUFACTURED IN THE UNITED STATES OF AMERICA

To Mary

Contents

I Had a Child Who Died

The bond among grieving parents is close. It is unfathomable. It cannot be entered into by outsiders, but it is known to each of us. A quick look, an acknowledgment, and we know immediately the agenda of suffering we have in common and that there is no fact of our lives more important than this: *I had a child who died.*

Over the months and years we will learn to say it more calmly. Yet each time we say it—and we must, it is a part of our learning our own terrible truth—the heart will jump, the stomach contract, the tempo of the body will shift in acknowledgment: I had a child who died.

But there is little to help us. It is not expected in our culture that children will die. Children grow up and become adults and perhaps marry and have children of their own, and they come home for Christmas, and they call us on Mother's Day and Father's Day. We get together and watch their children and reminisce how it was when they were small and we were younger. We pass on to them not only our genes—our blue eyes and the shape of our feet—but our ancestral pictures, our family recipes, our holiday customs, and when we are old and frail they will come to see us and love us. And we will leave *them*. They won't leave *us*.

And then it is over. It is not going to happen. We are in a shambles, wounded by the event of their death. With an ache that is physical and encompassing, we miss their presence now. And that space which in our fantasy they were to have filled until the end of our life is empty, and will be, until the end of our life. There will be others we love—other children, other smiles and tilts of head, other voices, but not theirs. And we wonder, How could so small a complex of blood and tissue, nerve and bone and love contain so much of our heart's lode?

It is an affront. It is a reversal of nature. It is terror. It is panic. It will break our heart. And for a while we think maybe that will happen. We, too, will die and be spared. We will flee away. And it will be over.

But life does not treat us like that. Nor, except in our worst moments, is that what we want. We do want life. There are other people who need us and whom we love. What we want is somehow to incorporate this most terrible event into our lives so we can be whole people again, weaving our scars and our memories and our stories and our hopes into the continuing fabric of our lives.

But how? Somehow if we know what something is, we can handle it better. Much of our pain seems a whirling jumble, and it is hard to know where to catch hold of it, to get it to stop long enough for us to sort out some of the confusing, painful feelings that preoccupy us or into which we stumble unexpectedly. The purpose of this book is to help us identify what is going on; then to give some suggestions of ways we can deal with grief; to give ways for us to begin, as we are ready and as we want, to rebuild our lives again; and to show how to do this in the context of the Christian faith.

 A Preliminary Word about Grief and the Christian Faith

Somehow we may have gotten the notion that real Christians are beyond grieving, that faith takes away the pain. It surely helps. There is no aspect of grieving and healing more important than faith, none that gives us more hope, more ability to cope, to rebuild. But, at the same time, our flesh aches for the flesh of our child, for that which we beheld with our eyes and touched with our hands. We would do less than honor to the creation of God if we did not mourn the loss of the riches God had given us in that child. If we need assurance that it is all right to cry, we can remember that at the grave of his friend Lazarus, "Jesus wept" (John 11:35). To be a Christian is to know something of the risks God has taken for love's sake. To be a parent is to know the risks we have taken for love's sake. We are not alone.

And we have promises: "Let not your hearts be troubled. . . . In my Father's house are many rooms. . . . I will not leave you desolate; I will come to you" (John 14:1,2,18). Or, in the words of the hymn "How Firm a Foundation":

> For I will be with thee thy troubles to bless,
> And sanctify to thee thy deepest distress.

But this will not happen unless we are willing, with the help of faith, to meet our child's death on its own anguishing terms, grieve over it, ask questions and, in time, allow it to become a part of our life's complex pattern.

Believing It—"I Can't Believe It Happened!"

The death of a child shakes our trust in the world at the most primal level. We know the world is full of disorder and catastrophe but, for the most part, we count on things happening reliably in our daily lives. Then, that which is so integral to our lives that it seems almost our reason for being, is taken away, gone. Our whole sense of ourselves is so disoriented and confused, the organizing patterns of our lives will not work anymore. Is it any wonder we "can't believe it"?

When a child dies after a long illness, there is time to prepare, though this has its own terror—the long waiting, the child's grief and pain, the debilitation and constraint that go with caring for a sick person, knowing how to face the child's fears and our own. But at least there is time to get used to the idea.

But when the death of a child happens quickly, in an accident or through violence of some kind, there is no time to prepare. Grief occupies one's life out to the edges, yet the central fact is wrong. We keep readjusting details, changing the scenario, imagining that something went differently. Perhaps when we turn the corner, wake up the next morning—it will all have been a mistake! We *know* better, but it is hard to *believe*.

The first days are terrible, the shock newest. We may want to turn away. We may think we don't want to see the child's body, that we cannot bear it. Our aversion is understandable but an unwise guide. Seeing is believing. Elisabeth Kübler-Ross, in an article in a leading woman's magazine, suggested that when possible the parents hold the body of the child, comb the child's hair, as a way of bringing some closure, acting out their relinquishment of the one they have so loved. She suggests there is a strange comfort in doing this: I have cared for this child in life, I am caring for her now that death has come.

In the first days, there is often a kind of numbness and a flurry of activity that keeps us from looking down the long hallways of despair and loss. People bring us food, they call, they expect us to cry. They are there for us in a wonderful and saving way. Religious services bring their own comfort, a kind of signification of our lives so that, for a while at least, we feel God is listening, loving us through others who stay close.

Then those days are gone. We have time alone, and the task of "believing it" may seem to dog our every effort to cope with the loss.

Our daughter died in an accident, in a fall from a horse. Weeks afterward, a friend who is also a therapist was visiting us from out of town. She had known our daughter, too, and loved her, and the intent of our friend's visit was to bring us what comfort and help she could. She asked members of our family what seemed to be our biggest stumbling block. When I said I kept thinking that if I looked long enough I'd find someone who'd tell me it wasn't so, she said, "Tell me about the day it happened." So I did, haltingly, at times overcome by tears. From time to time she would stop me, ask questions, nod, and if I expressed some thought about which I had misgivings, she would say, "Of course," giving me the permission I needed to own and accept my feelings. We went all the way through—morning, afternoon, the waiting, the knowing, the rest of the day, the terrors and the pain. And when at last, exhausted from the telling, I had finished, I felt as though some weight had gathered itself and lifted and had gone, and had left me to that extent released, more free. Not that the event was any less terrible, but at least I was not spending so much energy trying to deny the truth.

That was not the last time I was to go over in minute detail some of the events of that day, but it was the first. And it taught me something important about the process of grief, of learning to accept the unacceptable. When I spoke of this later to a young woman whose father had died suddenly three years before, she said, "Yes," and told me how it had not been until recently, long after her father's death, that she had gone through that day's events with someone she loved and how important and freeing that had been for her.

It is best if the friend who listens to the grievous retelling of such a day *not* be a family member or someone also heavily involved in the grief. It *is* comforting—an extra measure of support—if the friend we share our story with also shares in some measure our Christian faith. Though we may not even speak of it this time, we know the common hope is there.

Who's to Blame?

As our minds continue to churn over and over, as we try to make some sense out of the shambles our life has become, we may look for someone or something to blame. When things are so bad surely it's somebody's fault. "Who sinned," the disciples asked Jesus, "this man or his parents, that he was born blind?" (John 9:2).

Sometimes there *is* someone to blame, but even in a case so terrible as when a child is murdered, there is a blame beyond the specific cause of death which we seem to need to locate somewhere. We may ask, How did *God* allow this to happen? It is our rage at the universe; of course, we are angry. We haven't done anything to deserve so great a blow.

It is a question as old as thought. It is Job's question: "I was at ease, and he [God] broke me asunder. . . . My face is red with weeping, and on my eyelids is deep darkness; although there is no violence in my hands, and my prayer is pure" (Job 16:12,16,17). And God, after hearing him out, says, in effect, "Wait. Wait, Job. You don't know what I know." And Job realizes that, in truth, he doesn't understand the ways of God and, *having expressed his anger and puzzlement,* is able to settle for the fact that he cannot know God's ways, and is, in time, restored and able to trust God again.

15

Perhaps it is so for us, too. Can we be relieved of the burden of thinking that through the death of our child somehow God was singling us out for pain? It is hard, indeed, to keep from hating God no matter how much we think we shouldn't, and yet believe that God is present in the meaning and pain and hope of everything we encounter. Can we believe that, as the old song puts it, "We'll understand it better by and by"? "Now we see in a mirror dimly," Paul says, "but then face to face. Now I know in part; then I shall understand fully, even as I have been fully understood" (1 Cor. 13:12).

We blame ourselves, though there may be no reason to. We all have feelings of unworthiness, guilts we have accumulated over the years. They stand on the ready, waiting for some insecurity to trigger them and send them down upon us. We read how a small child who loses a loved one has feelings of guilt: Because I have sometimes been angry with that person, wished him out of the way, it is my fault that he has died. This misplaced guilt is something adults, too, have to deal with. If there has been some element of neglect or possible poor judgment (such as the gift of a motorcycle in which the youngster then has a fatal accident), it is easier to understand. But even if there is no way we can inflict ourselves with any fragment of responsibility, the guilt feelings may come.

A parent's most basic job is to preserve the safety of

the child. This is my child, I am responsible for her. It is my fault that I could not save her. My own feeling that somehow I *failed* her was made more difficult by the fact that as a child I had suffered from a long, dangerous illness—and my mother had nursed me through. My mother had been able to save me. Why could I not do as much for my daughter?

These are irrational fears. What has happened is over. If we *are* in some way guilty, perhaps we can remember Jesus' admonition to Peter that he forgive "seventy times seven" (Matt. 18:22). Would God do less for us?

We may feel guilty at not being "good grievers." We berate ourselves: Where is our faith? Where is our trust in God that we continue to feel so despondent? We have a hard time concentrating. We break down and cry perhaps even in public! So we may lay an extra load of guilt on our already-burdened heart because we're not "managing" any better, not being a better "witness" for the power of faith to overcome sorrow.

What's to "manage"? We have been terribly hurt. Of course we're sad. God manages. We are creatures. We do our best. We need to bring our feelings to the surface and let them out or they will fester and cost us more in the end. Tears are a relief, and so are cries of anger, even when there is no one to be angry with. Listen to the psalmist:

17

> I am so troubled that I cannot speak.
> I consider the days of old,
> I remember the years long ago. . . .
> "Will the Lord spurn forever,
> and never again be favorable?"
>
> —Psalm 77:4,5,7

Then, and maybe only then, is the psalmist able to remember the good things: "I will call to mind the deeds of the Lord: yea, I will remember thy wonders of old" (Psalm 77:11).

It takes a very long time—years, not weeks or months—to feel less than overwhelming sadness at the death of one's child.

As for inflicting our sorrow on other people, one does not want to go around blathering and crying all the time. But perhaps it is our gift to others to trust them enough to share our feelings with them. It may help them deal with some of their own. If we can choose where to cry, at home or with a few people who will be fully understanding, perhaps we will feel easier. But if we can't—if we are in church and a hymn catches us off guard, or at a football game and we remember being there with a son or daughter now gone—well, the earth is our home and we can cry where we want. (It may be helpful to remember that Jesus cried out in anguish in the midst of a jeering and unsympathetic multitude.)

We'll feel better in time, and in less time if we are able to express our sadness. If we do not open a wound to the air, it is harder for the wound to heal. If we do not surface our grief, it cannot move away from us, leaving us ready for new life. We need to be gentle with ourselves, as we would be with a wounded child.

Living with the Unfinished Business

The child's life seems prematurely cut off, as well as our own work of parenting. But we also grieve for what we were "in the midst of" that never got completed.

If a child has a lingering illness, as with an adult, there may be opportunity to say to one another what we need to say before the chance is lost. But there may not be time or opportunity. Certainly if death is quick and unexpected, there is not time. We are left holding a handful of yarn, threads to weave, and the fabric is torn away. There are things going on between us and the child—things we may want to apologize for, inequities we would like to correct. Little things, many of them . . . "That time I took your brother to lunch by himself—I was going to take you another time and I didn't. I'm sorry." . . . "That time I yelled at you for breaking my mother's vase—it wasn't that important, at all." Angers to express, if we can face them . . . "That time you said I never paid attention to you—why, I've spent half my life. . . !" And on, and on.

I suppose there is no instance of unfinished business more grievous than the suicide of one's child. It isn't fair of the child to just walk away, to desert us. Of course, we're angry. Yet we want to tell the child, "I love you. You must have been feeling terrible. If only you had told us." We blame ourselves. We go over and over our last conversations, looking for clues, interposing something that would have stopped the child, made it all right. But there is no answer, and no way of straightening it out. We come to the wall and cannot pass through. We are left there, shouting into nothing.

The resources of faith can help us—our knowledge that we are all imperfect and all forgiven, our faith that someday we will be with our loved one, that the relationship is not over, and that it has not ended forever on this terrible note. We may also need the help of a professional therapist. There are organizations in some cities where families of suicide victims can meet together and talk.

Whatever the circumstances of our child's death, we may be tempted to idealize the relationship we had with the child because the unfinished business is so painful. Our own daughter died at sixteen. A friend whose daughter had been through a tumultuous adolescence said to me, "I couldn't have stood it if Betsy had died at that age. We were always fighting, half the time we didn't speak to each other. If she had died in the midst of that. . . ."

Too quickly, I said, "Oh no, it wasn't like that for us. We were very close. We had a wonderful relationship." Which we did, but it had a lot of tension in it, too. Our daughter was struggling to establish her independence and there had been occasions of hurt and anger between us. But it wasn't until months had passed that I was fully able to acknowledge the difficulties there had been in a relationship that basically was fine.

It is unwise, because it is untrue, to idealize the dead. It is in no one's interest. We will spend a lot of needed energy keeping that illusion in place. We may need it for a while, perhaps, as a buffer to help us learn our new life a piece at a time. But if we persist in some idealization of our child, we cannot face the rest of our realities either, and we will not honor the vigor and truth of the child who has died. We will not believe ourselves, and those who know us and remember the child best will not believe us either. The myth of perfection is hard to maintain. We do not need it. We can give it over—to God, if we will. Lay it down. Leave it there. The child, as he or she was, was God's child, acceptable, loved, all right. And so are we.

Being Able to Let Go

How hard it is! The physical letting go has already happened. Against our will, our child was taken from us.

But there is a much longer letting go that must take place if we are to reenter life on its terms. Since those terms are the only ones available to us, we have no other choice. Still, we resist. We play "if only" games with ourselves, trying to change the unchangeable, trying to pretend it isn't so. We become newly possessive of our child, brooding over our memories and thoughts. We may even, in thought and preoccupation, try to follow the child into death, until we realize after a while that we cannot do it, and we turn back. Still, our thoughts move toward the child as metal to a magnet.

Why is it so hard to let go? This is, in one way, an outrageous question. The child is flesh of our flesh. It is as though a part of our own body is torn away. We mourn what we have lost. We counted on the child's being with us throughout life. Of course it's hard!

The task of letting go has different meanings depending on the age of the child who died. Parents whose child dies at birth have the terrible void of hardly knowing the child at all. For the mother, the physical loss of something so recently of her own body makes her feel this death is the loss of part of her most intimate self.

All the expected joy of infancy and new parenting, the preparation of furniture and clothing that now will not be used, the eagerness of family and friends to speculate on what the child will be like—these must all be modulated back into lives in which the new central character is suddenly gone, without ever really becoming known.

At the other extreme is the parent who in old age loses a child who also is well past maturity. One of the most wrenching sights of my life was sitting at a graveside and seeing a woman of nearly ninety sob at the burial of her daughter, dead at sixty-five. Parents should die first, not children. One recapitulates whatever life the child has had and, in anguish and tenderness, must give the child up.

But maybe it will help us to "come to life" again if we can take up some of the aspects of our resistance, hold them in our hands, turn them around and, maybe, by the grace of God, put them down. Not throw them away—we have lost enough already—but put them on some shelf of the mind or in some notebook or journal so they will be there if we want to look at them again, but where they will be less active, less demanding, less puzzling.

We have looked at some of them already. I will refer to them again.

It is hard to let go because of our guilt—not only for real or imagined wrongdoing, but simply for surviving.

Those who have studied the aftereffects of terrible events, such as the holocaust or disastrous fires, speak of the guilt of the survivor. We are alive and the child is dead. We are guilty.

It is hard to let go because of our unfinished business: the things we planned to say, the developments we trusted to occur. We are left standing, the unfinished business in our outstretched hands and no one to reach toward us to help us finish it, "straighten it out."

It is hard to let go because, like an amputee whose leg is gone, our muscles of parenting continue to twitch, to move us toward tasks for which there is no recipient—the place at the table we continue to set, the car that is always too big for the family, or the times we find ourselves counting over one too many seats at the movies.

The Long View—Looking ahead to Loss

Our "muscles of parenting" have been developed and in use, in most instances, for many years. We had expected to need them with this child for a long time, though in changing form. It is as though we had a basketful of parent/child exchanges and we are left, then, with our child prematurely leaving us and the basket still in our hands. A bereaved mother said, "But I'm not *finished* yet, being her mother!" So we dive into the basket, turning up what we will not be able to use, wondering what to do with all the energy we had invested in our future with this child, grieving not only for our present loss, but for all the unknown experiences we would have had together in the years to come. There will be many; it is understandable that we should feel this way. When his daughter died, Mark Twain said he felt like the man who, watching his house burn down, said it would be years before he knew everything he had lost.

It is understandable, but after a while it is not wise and perhaps we can let it go. Sufficient unto the day are the griefs of the day. The grandchildren we will not have, the intimacy we will not have with this child are wounding to contemplate. But at least we know the outlines of the terrors ahead. Sometimes it is hard to let go because, having been so stricken with this loss, we look anxiously ahead thinking something worse will happen. With this child, the worst *has* happened. We do not need to fear heartbreaking illness or disaster, further terrors, anything!

It is dark comfort and is not intended as comfort at all. It is only to say that if we have trouble letting go because of some inchoate fear that something worse will happen down the road, we can perhaps release that fear. It won't. If our faith means anything, it means the child is safe, with God.

As for ourselves, we do, as the song says, live one day at a time. None of us knows what the years ahead might have held. During the rest of our lives, each day brings its share of roads not taken, of options no longer possible. We don't even know whether we will be alive in those years we had anticipated. "Do not be anxious about tomorrow, for tomorrow will be anxious for itself. Let the day's own trouble be sufficient for the day" (Matt. 6:34).

The Short View

What about the day's own trouble? For each day has its recurrent demands that we acknowledge the child is gone, and that we let go. Still, we go on responding— involuntarily, almost—as though the child were in our care.

We are parents; our job is to look out for our children. What if they need us? What if they are lonely or scared? What if they feel abandoned that we are not with them? What if they look around heaven and they don't see us? These are childlike, earthbound images, but we are children when it comes to understanding the mysteries of death. And we remember how it feels to be frightened and alone, and we know we have comforted our children before in the face of strange, new events.

27

Then we tell ourselves: God knows their need, God will care for them, be their mother and their father. And we try to put flesh and bones on the idea of infinite love, infinite caring. How to think about it? "Saints in glory"? "In my Father's house are many rooms"? "The dead shall be raised incorruptible"? The details can wait, and must, yet we do need ways to think of our children as being received into love before we can let them go.

In grappling with my own anxiety I talked with my pastor. Even as I knew it was *my* need I was expressing, I couldn't seem to shake the thought, What if she needs me?

He said, "Remember at the memorial service for Mary, the love in the room, so thick you could almost put your hand out and touch it?" Indeed I did, and the friend at the service who stood up and spoke of it—"I wish to bear witness to the love that is in this room"—and my own feeling of being surrounded by love, by a transcending peace and joy, a climate so rich and transforming nothing could hurt any of us.

"Yes, I do," I said.

My pastor went on to say that perhaps such experiences are foretastes, or hints, of a greater life with God. We sat there together remembering, and then he said, "So if it's anything like *that*," he hesitated and, with tears of relief, I finished the sentence, "then Mary's all right."

I have gone back to that moment many times, remembering. We need images of comfort, of joy, of happy arrival for our children before we can relinquish our parenting and begin to let them go. Elisabeth Kübler-Ross says it is her belief that none of us dies alone, that someone we love always comes to meet us. A friend, whose father had died not long before, wrote to us after our child's death, "My dad will look out for Mary." It was wonderfully comforting.

Letting our children go. Are we afraid we'll forget, that time will dim the memory of our precious child, that somehow over the years we'll let someone or something else occupy the space that was theirs? We need not worry. As theologian Dietrich Bonhoeffer wrote in *Letters and Papers from Prison:*

Nothing can fill the gap when we are away from those we love, and it would be wrong to try and find anything. We must simply hold out and win through. That sounds very hard at first, but at the same time it is a great consolation, since leaving the gap unfilled preserves the bond between us. It is nonsense to say that God fills the gap; he does not fill it, but keeps it empty so that our communion with another may be kept alive, even at the cost of pain.

Perhaps as parents must let their adolescent children go, in the faith that they will return under new terms, so we may be able to relinquish our children into death, hoping that in ways we do not foresee they may return to be with us, to bless us with their presence.

 Letting Go of the Grief Event

This is different from letting the child go, though at first they are all wound together. It is helpful, as we are able, to separate the two.

It's easy to see why we don't want to open our hand and let the grief event go, whether it is a lingering illness or a sudden, violent death. It is the last place we knew the child and, of course, we want to hold onto it. It calls us to its presence, the great dividing moment between life and death.

If death was sudden and violent, then we must add that to the other burdens of our loss. We are preoccupied with it, though we may express that by turning resolutely away. We cannot let it go. We go through the event, or around it, torturing ourselves. How did the child *feel?*

Eventually we will have to face these terrors down or we will not heal. Again, in studies of mass death events, we learn that those who come through best are those who are able to go over the terrifying details until they somehow "get used to it." It is the same with us. We must face our terrors, bring them to the surface, talk about them, or we will be imprisoned and cannot go free.

If we are still having trouble believing it, we may also cling to the grief event as a way of trying to hold back time. If we dig in at the moment before our child died, maybe we can change it, make it turn out differently. "I do not agree," we say to life. "I do not concede. I do not accept what has happened. You are wrong."

Grief is also exhausting, it is labor, and we have limits to our strength. For us to begin to let go is to open ourselves to other burdens. We have to *decide* what to pay attention to and, for a while at least, we don't have the strength for that. There is a kind of narrowing of the field of vision, since our grief is all we care about, almost all we know. We may be impatient when someone tries to tell us of troubles in some far-off land. Don't tell me, I have troubles enough of my own; my quota of suffering is filled. It is hard to let go of our simple, consuming loss.

But the world will not stand still for us, nor will the course of events reverse and go differently the next time. In *Hour of Gold, Hour of Lead*, Anne Morrow Lindbergh quotes Laurens Van der Post as saying:

31

One of the most pathetic things about us human beings is our touching belief that there are times when the truth is not good enough for us; that it can and must be improved upon. We have to be utterly broken before we can realize that it is impossible to better the truth. It is the truth that we deny which so tenderly and forgivingly picks up the fragments and puts them together again.

Letting Go of the Things

It is heartbreaking to go through closets and drawers and decide what to do with the clothes and toys and books of a child who has died. But it is not wise to keep these things around as they were. We need to act out for ourselves the reality of the child's death.

We will not want to part with everything. Or do it all at once. But we should begin soon. I could not bring myself to take my child's clothing and dump it into a collection box in a shopping center. We found a friend who was operating a perpetual garage sale, the proceeds of which were to go to children overseas. We gave her many of our daughter's clothes. Another friend in a distant city who had several daughters was the recipient of a box or two. We saved some books, a few items of clothing, some pictures, the journals and poems our daughter had written. But the house is not a shrine. A few mementos are better than reminders everywhere. The rest of the family is here, too. Some special treasures—a ring, a sixpence to be worn in a bridal shoe, a leather box with her name tooled in gold—we saved for occasions yet to come, to pass along as our daughter's gift to the living, as she would have liked.

The Rest of the Family

The loss of a child is a great grief for the whole family, yet each of us has our own special burden. We are drawn closer. We are also plunged more deeply into ourselves. While we are bonded together, in our suffering each of us is alone.

How do we meet one another's needs? We cannot, not completely. There is much we can do for each other—talking, holding one another close, being together. But after the first days and weeks, when we are so sensitized to one another it seems we almost breathe in unison, the paths of our emotional needs will begin to diverge. We may find ourselves hurt and angry and confused that those with whom we share so great a loss sometimes seem distant, preoccupied, not able to help us.

We need to remember that the agenda of grief is as individual as the people who grieve. Each of us has different items of unfinished business. A mother may feel a child's loss almost as a physical cutting away of a part of herself; a father may brood over the fact that he wasn't closer to the child, and now the child is gone. We also have different ways of dealing with grief. A mother may be more overt in her grief. A father may plunge more resolutely into work. They may not understand each other.

The loss of a child is a dangerous time for a marriage. One expert has said that in 75 percent of the families where a child has died, the marriage is in serious trouble within a year. It isn't only the issues surrounding the death of the child that can cause trouble. It is also all the other incompletely resolved issues in our lives that may have been tolerable when things were going well. Now, as with any life-altering crisis, they spring out into the open again, demanding attention. We are already burdened. We are ill equipped to deal with old troubles, yet here they come.

We may need counseling to help us through. If the marriage survives and some of the old issues, in the wake of this crucible of grief, are brought to a better resolution, the marriage will be richer and closer. The blessing of the child who has died will be felt in the refreshed lives of husband and wife—a legacy of love.

The surviving children in the family also have special needs. They have some of the same problems the parents have—guilt, unfinished business, the struggle for faith. And they have fewer years to have gained the perspectives of time. Yet, as parents, we are often so preoccupied with our own grief we do not realize the children are needing us badly. A surprising number of children who have experienced the death of a brother or sister report feelings of being uncared about, that no one had time to listen to their grief. We may even try to exclude them, in some vain effort to spare them pain. The kinds of sharing possible depend on the ages of the children and on their own wishes. But certainly they need to be included as grievers, to have our attention to their suffering, our sensitive appreciation and gratitude for their continuing presence in our lives.

Grandparents, too, need to be included in the family's grieving. They have not only the loss of a grandchild to bear, but the pain of their own child in so terrible a loss.

Where Can We Go for Help?

As Christians, we go to the carriers of the faith. We go to the church, the minister, the services; those in the congregation to whom we're close; the stories, the rituals, that speak of Christian hope in the face of death; the words of scripture that echo the faith of centuries.

One of the most helpful letters we received after our daughter's death began by simply quoting the two verses of Paul from the book of Romans: "For I am sure that neither death, nor life, nor angels, nor principalities, nor things present, nor things to come, nor powers, nor height, nor depth, nor anything else in all creation, will be able to separate us from the love of God in Christ Jesus our Lord" (Rom. 8:38,39).

The community of believers offers loving arms, and shoulders to cry on, their presence a witness to their faith, their words a message of consolation. We rest in their presence and feel secure. Surely God must love us if God's people love us so much. The church is there for us, and, over the years, the rituals and witness of the church and community will, we hope, continue to be a vehicle through which we can find joy and hope.

But if, in a few weeks, the attention of the community moves on to someone else or assumes we are now "feeling better" and they are fearful of upsetting us by bringing up the subject of our loss, what then? Congregations differ greatly in their sensitivity to continuing hurt, and in letting people know the church is a place we can bring our pain and it will be received compassionately, and without embarrassment. We will always have the rituals of the church to be our comfort, to remind us of who we are, and the prayers of the faithful to help sustain us. But we will need more than this, too. For our needs for understanding may be greater, not less, as time goes by and the truth of our loss drags through day after day and new seasons bring new griefs, new evidences of loss. Christmas. Birthdays. Anniversaries. The first day of school. The whole round of the year with its "first time" for everything.

We need one or two friends—someone outside our family circle who does not share our grief in such a devastating way—to stand with us, to be a sounding board as we struggle through our thoughts, to listen as we go over again and again the anguish we feel. During the week after the memorial service for our daughter, a friend who had a son she had to pick up each day during a week's sessions of basketball camp, called me every day before she set out. "Would you like to ride along with me?" Every day I went with her, and we would leave a little early and stop and sit under a tree, or go for a Coke. And I would talk—incoherently, sometimes, usually with tears—about sorrow and dreams and my daughter and the hard moments since yesterday. Each time she would drop me off at home I would feel as if, for a while, I had been purged of the day's accumulation of pain, the daily interest of a wound which would never go away but which through this draining off of the day's terrors was, perhaps, already beginning to heal. It was almost a physical thing, this release of the pressure of grief, just as one loosens the lid on a can and hears the pressure escape.

That was years ago and I no longer need that kind of daily attention. But it was a gift beyond measure when it was offered and, in the ensuing years, I have had occasion to be grateful to that friend and to a few others who "heard me out" when I needed to talk. (In time, we became such friends ourselves).

Sometimes, with the best of intentions, friends don't know how to help. They may feel that to bring up the subject of our loss is to risk making us feel worse; so they avoid it and talk of other things while the presence of the unspoken builds to almost intolerable pressure. Or, they may think that to divert our attention to something else is an act of kindness.

We may need to help them, to break through the facade of well-intentioned pleasantries, and say, "I need to talk about what's going on with me." Often they will be grateful, and the sharing of our grief may help them deal with their own vicarious sorrow at our pain, as well as their own uneasiness about the matter of death. Much of the uneasiness in talking about a friend's grief is our own anxiety about death.

Many months after our tragedy, we would occasionally see friends who did not know of our loss. If they were close enough to us, we would tell them. Such experiences, far from being awkward because they were so long after the fact, were a relief to us. We were able to speak again of our grief and loss which to them, and to us, still seemed fresh and raw, whereas others might treat it as far more "resolved" than we felt it to be.

We found that our circle of friends shifted somewhat after our child's death. We were surprised and disappointed that people we thought were good friends became distant, uneasy, and seemed unable to help us. Others who were casual acquaintances became suddenly close, sustainers of life for us. Grief changes the rules, and sometimes rearranges the combinations. Perhaps those who became close are more able to deal with death and grief. Perhaps in some way they need us, too. My husband and I have become like second parents to a young woman who needs us, and she has become almost a daughter to us.

There are, beyond friends, beyond our church, other people and agencies in the community that can help. Most communities have counseling centers and mental health centers. They usually operate with fees on a sliding scale related to ability to pay, so the expense of counseling is not prohibitive. Even if we don't feel we are in desperate need, it may be a good idea to go once, or a few times, for the support and security it may give us. Sometimes it helps us to be sure we are moving in the right direction in handling our grief—as one would go to a doctor for a physical checkup.

The help of supportive groups cannot be over-stressed. Any group where there is genuine love and caring will help—a bridge group, a Bible study group, a biweekly meeting of friends. But it is also helpful, at least for a period of time, to be in a group that meets regularly and is more intentional in encouraging people to deal with their feelings—a therapy group, a grief group. There are networks of groups across the country whose purpose is expressly to help parents who have had children die. A list of several such groups is given at the end of this book, along with a short list of books which are helpful.

There are many ways we can help ourselves toward healing, toward rebirth. For a Christian, surely faith is a help we turn to, both at the onset of our grief and as the months and years unfold. But, as was said earlier, we need to bring our whole lives into the stream of faith, sometimes to hurl ourselves in anger at the feet of God, not just to come in resignation or in tender supplication. "Are you afraid to be angry with God?" one therapist asks. "Why? Don't you think God can take it?"

So, how to pray? How to try to relate to God when the universe seems to have dealt us such a body blow? When our whole sense of the order and reliability of life is thrown up in our face?

We can pray in gratitude for the past, for our memories, for what we have been given of the child which will never leave us. This may seem hard to do when we feel such pain about the child's leaving. But it is also comforting to know that what we have experienced together in the past is inviolate; though the future as we had expected it is gone from us, the past is not gone. We are still the child's parents.

We can bring God our grief and sometimes our despair, not with apologies attached but as a child brings fears to a parent: "Here I am. Hold me. Take care of me."

We can bring God our emptiness and say, "Fill me." And then wait, attentively, in hope. We can bring God our panic, "What do I do now? What will save me?" Perhaps, in our listening, a thought comes to our mind. Maybe I should call a friend. Maybe I should call the minister. Maybe I should sit here and cry for a while, or read the book someone lent me yesterday, or walk out among the flowers or the dark trees, or write something down in a journal. We can follow these "intimations of the spirit" and see where they will lead us. A poem of Galway Kinnell, "How Many Nights," came to our house the Christmas after our daughter was killed. It seemed like a message, sent to me:

How many nights
have I lain in terror,
O Creator Spirit, Maker of night and day,

only to walk out
the next morning over the frozen world
hearing under the creaking of snow

faint, peaceful breaths . . .
snake,
bear, earthworm, ant . . .

and above me
a wild crow crying *'yaw yaw yaw'*
from a branch nothing cried from ever in my life.

Is the arrival of a poem an answer to prayer? Or finding, while browsing through the Psalms, a passage that exactly echoes our thoughts? Or the unexpected and desperately-needed arrival of a friend at the door? Or a phone call when we are feeling desolate? Perhaps. How does God answer our prayers, comfort our distress? We are desperate for signs, but we do not want to be fools, victims of our self-delusion.

Frederick Buechner, in a wonderful book *The Alphabet of Grace*, has this to say:

We are all of us more mystics than we believe. . . .
Through some moment of beauty or pain, some
sudden turning of our lives, through some horror
of the twelve o'clock news, some dream, some
breakfast on the first and last of all our days, we

catch glimmers at least of what the saints are blind-
ed by. Only then, unlike the saints . . . we tend to
go on as though nothing has happened. To go on as
though something *has* happened even though we
are not sure what it was or just where we are sup-
posed to go with it, is to enter that dimension of life
that religion is a word for.

Often, when things are going well for us, we don't pay
attention to these "glimmers" of what the saints have
seen. As grieving parents, sensitized to the world of the
spirit, praying, attentive, watching with the eyes of
faith, they can be lights in our darkness, God holding a
parent's loving arms to us: See, I am here. I have not left
you. Come now, all shall be well.

There are other things we can do for ourselves besides
these ventures of the spirit. Simple, physical things, like
getting enough exercise, sleep, the right food. Getting a
physical checkup, if we haven't for a while—periods of
grief are notorious for more-frequent-than-usual inci-
dents of physical illness.

We can be a little more resistant to calls of duty,
though responsibilities, too, can help us keep going. But
if we usually tend to be super-conscientious, we can re-
lax a little. If we have a choice, we can be with people
who lift our spirits. Do something for ourselves. A
friend told me that when she began to sew some spring

clothes for herself, she began to feel better—a kind of belief in life again.

We should find some balance between solitude and socializing, both of which we need. People will urge socializing upon us. "You need to get out," they will say. We do need to get out in order to reestablish ourselves as persons who belong to life and to current relationships. But we also need time alone, to face our demons, to put down our plumbline and to take our soundings. We will probably cry, feel sad. We will also feel alive and enriched and less tense because we have looked our grief in the face, allowed our feelings to speak their authentic word. And when we move out again into the social world, it may be with a sense of having laid some burden down.

When we do go into social groups, we need not expect too much of ourselves or feel we have to be scintillating or muster up the small talk. We can let someone else worry about that for a while.

Part of what we are telling ourselves in these bits of self-affirmation and even indulgence is, *I am worthwhile.* This is important in counteracting that primordial feeling: because my child has died, I must have failed. I was made aware of the depth of my need for reassurance when we received, after our daughter's death, a greeting card with a poem that began, "Love yourself. . . . Value your attributes. . . . Appreciate

your gifts." I responded to that card as a drowning person gasps for air. For months I kept it taped to my wall
and read it over and over, and it made me realize how
desperately we need reassuring when a child has suddenly died, that life itself is not rejecting us. It is not a
reasonable reaction at all, but the death of a child is not
reasonable, either.

Keeping the Energy of Grief Moving

It is important in dealing with all aspects of grief that
we keep the process moving. The temptation when
one's child has died is to freeze, to stay perpetually on
the recoil in a kind of arrested cringe against so terrible
a blow. I remember feeling, months after my daughter's
death, as though I were still on occasions flung back
against a wall, reeling from a blow. Some people stay in
that psychic state, shrinking inward (a psychic acting
out of physical recoil), a crusting over of the self to de-
fend against ever being struck like that again. We all
perhaps have known or heard of people like this, who,
twenty years later, still live at the occasion of their
grief, a terrible but familiar "sulk" against life. It is understandable but unwise, and we and our loved ones
will suffer. Our sulking will not cause some cosmic

presence to see the error of its ways and come around at last to offer us our child again.

No, after the first terrible recoil when for a few days the blood seems almost to stand still in the veins, we must let down our guard and let the processes of grief and life begin to move through us again. Just as physical wounds will not heal without a ready motion of blood to nourish and carry away, the wounds of grief will not heal without a psychic flow moving through the grieving person and out to whatever persons and projects are there to help us deal with grief.

How to keep this process going? We already have mentioned friends to talk with, and prayer. Another way to keep the grief moving is to write it down. In the year after my daughter's death, I filled four notebooks with entries—writing sometimes daily, sometimes several times a day, sometimes only once in several days. I described feelings, the events of the day, occasions of recall, of sorrow or hope. It was a means of moving the grief away, getting it down somewhere else, siphoning it off. A friend whose son committed suicide told me what a helpful milestone it was when she sat down and made two lists, one of "bad things" and one of "good things" about her son's life. She related how she felt better as she saw the few entries in the first list and the long list of "good things." Writer Isak Dinesen once said if you can write it down or if you can put it in a story, anything is bearable.

To read the works of others who have gone through grief is another way of keeping the process going, and of finding another understanding friend. When a writer describes for me how I am feeling, she or he becomes my friend; I am not alone. Somehow that person has achieved some peace with the pain, enough to write it down. Maybe, I, too, will find my way through this.

We will begin to find others who have had more recent experiences of loss than ours. If we reach out to them, it will help us both.

In trying to keep our grief moving, we need to look at all of our other relationships. The relationships of our life are a system, an interlocking network, and when one element is affected so are they all. The death of a child will unbalance the whole lot—not only relationships with spouse and remaining children, but with all the people who are important in our lives. It is a good time to pay attention, to make these relationships as good as possible. If we are buoyed and fed by satisfying relationships now, there is less other-directed energy floating around, trying to attach in unrealistic ways to the one who is gone.

The relationship with the child who is dead must move, too, though we may not want that and we may cling to the image we last knew as a way of "holding on." Once, when I was talking with my husband about my persistent fantasy that by moving on I was abandoning my daughter, leaving her back there at the occasion of her death, he said, "But Mary isn't back there. That's not where she is. She has moved on 'from strength to strength' and I have to do that, too, to keep up with her." Maybe we can think of ourselves and our child as moving along some kind of parallel tracks and, therefore, closer to one another than we could ever be if we continued to hover around the event of the child's death. "Why do you seek the living among the dead?" (Luke 24:5), the angels asked the women at the tomb. "He is not here; for he has risen, as he said. . . . he is going before you to Galilee; there you will see him" (Matt. 28:6, 7).

Some Balancing Acts

Of course it is not all motion. "For everything there is a season," writes the author of Ecclesiastes:

a time to break down, and a time to build up;
a time to weep, and a time to laugh;
a time to mourn, and a time to dance . . .
a time to seek, and a time to lose;
a time to keep and a time to cast away.
—Ecclesiastes 3:4,6

So it is with us in our grieving. There must be times for standing still, for letting the full power of our grief come to the surface, be acknowledged; then, gently, as we are able, to move away from the grief. There will be times when we seem to have no choice, others when we can choose. I remember the moment when, in the grocery store several weeks after my daughter's death, I decided to "look cheerful" instead of continuing to walk around with a glum face. As grieving parents, we have lost so much, and it is hard to let go of anything, even our pain. We don't need to worry; it will be there again when we look for it.

It is helpful to realize, too, that an experience can contain both pain and joy—that it's not just one or the other. Perhaps one of the other children gets married. It is an occasion for joy. It also has its painful undertone that the child who died isn't there the way we'd like. Pain and joy—they are often two sides of a coin. To open ourselves to one is to receive the other also.

 When We Start to Feel Better

When do we start to feel better, to feel that life seems more important than death? There are, one hopes, moments of joy and peace, surprising gifts, from the very beginning: a hug and shared tears with a friend who really seems to understand; some sense of God's love that for a moment takes the pain away; release in floods of tears and a piece of music on the record player; a poem that speaks to us.

But these times are exceptions—for weeks, months, maybe even years. One psychologist suggests it takes seven years to recover from the death of someone close. At first we don't want to feel better. It seems like capitulation to an event we do not find acceptable. It seems disloyal! How can we "feel better" when our child is dead? Yet, the will of the mind and body and spirit is for health. If we allow grief to run its course for us, if we acknowledge the truth and submit to its wisdom, we will, in time, begin to feel better. At the time of the assassination of Martin Luther King, Jr., Robert Kennedy, still grieving for his own brother and now for King, quoted these words from Aeschylus: "In our sleep, pain which cannot forget falls drop by drop upon the heart until, in our own despair, against our will, comes wisdom through the awful grace of God."

So, we begin to feel better. At first this, too, is hard to believe. We never expected it, so it comes doubly as a gift.

Yet strangely enough, when we begin to feel better, some of the old battles we thought we had won come out of the shadows to demand another go-around. To forget for a while means to be stabbed with fresh aware-

ness when something calls our loss to mind again. The old questions return: How can I go on with new adventures and excitements when I have been so sad, when my child is gone? They come back like old songs. We must confront them all over, meet them on whatever terms this version contains, and, having done that, gently lay them aside.

We will need to keep our resources available, on the ready—though we may need them less constantly now—our friendships, our journal, maybe, our groups, our prayer in whatever form it takes, listening, asking, rejoicing, crying.

Whereas previously our moods seemed simply sad with occasional patches of light, now we may find an unsettling variation in our feelings, as happy times seem engrossing and satisfying, and then we are plunged into sadness again. Perhaps we can learn to accept these mood swings, recognizing the reality of each, knowing light gives way to darkness and darkness to light.

We will find ourselves drawn in an immediate bond to others who have suffered as we have. We may take the initiative, now that we are stronger and able to reach toward those still immobilized in the daze of first grief. Or they may turn to us, in trust and sorrow, before we know their need. About a year after our daughter died, a friend in a distant city called us one morning. Her son had just died suddenly. "Now it's happened to me!" she said. We are part of a community of suffering in which all are grievers, all are helpers.

"The meaning of original sin," declares theologian Robert Capon, "is that we would rather sulk than rejoin the party." Bit by slow and tender bit we stop holding out for better terms and start to "rejoin the party," knowing that we will carry our loss with us forever but that the patches of light are—can it be?—becoming greater than the patches of darkness.

We may experience, in these days of recovering, a loss of intensity as we shift our consciousness from the agenda of our suffering to new ventures and new concerns around us. Whereas before, we may have felt the presence of God at every turn, we may feel that less strongly now and may wonder whether we are losing touch with our source of power.

We need, of course, to keep open the channels of prayer, worship, reading, meditation, going around with our eyes open to the signs and wonders of creation. But it is understandable, now that our need is not so severe, that, like a wound that begins to heal and is less sensitive to every wafting breeze, we do not notice so readily every breath of the Spirit. It is all right. It is God's gift to us of healing, of steadiness, of confidence that whatever happens "the eternal God is thy refuge, and underneath are the everlasting arms" (Deut. 33:27, KJV).

The Rest of Our Life

What shall we hope for, we for whom at times "the rest of our life" seems a burden? We speak of death and rebirth. Is it possible that we who have experienced the death of a part of ourselves can also be reborn into "the rest of our life"? Do we want to? In most cases, if we want to, we can.

The pain of loss will not leave us. It will be less startling, less apt to take us by surprise—the feeling of a trap door opening beneath our feet. We will somehow weave it into the pattern of what our lives have been, who we are. It will, however, continue to catch us off guard, to stab us afresh. "How many children do you have?" "All sons? No daughters?" Sometimes we are glad for the questions. We want to be able to speak of our child, to tell who we are. The words of a song, the sight of a falling leaf on a vulnerable day, the family occasions of anniversaries, weddings, graduations, the welcome but poignant visits with our child's old friends, times when we feel sorry for ourselves and all our griefs are multiplied—any of these can make us feel the pain as though it were fresh. We would not, indeed, want this syndrome of pain and recall out of our lives because, were it to go, our ability to savor our life in its joy also would be diminished as would our ability to experience our child in ways that *are* possible.

What are they? Certainly, as we have said, the gifts of memory which, over time, do become occasions for joy, for laughter, though they always have the underside of loss. "What is essential does not die but clarifies," wrote Thornton Wilder. A father whose daughter was found to have a terminal illness said to his minister soon after the discovery, "I'd rather have had her for the years we have than never to have had her at all." Years later, when the child's illness had run its course and the height of grief had passed, the minister recalled those words to the father and told him how much they had meant to him. To which the father responded, "I felt that way then and I feel that way now, but there was a while when grief took over." All of us who have had children die know that journey well.

I will not leave you desolate; I will come to you. . . . because I live, you will live also. . . . Peace I leave with you; my peace I give to you; not as the world gives do I give to you. Let not your hearts be troubled, neither let them be afraid. . . . I go away, and I will come to you.

—John 14:18,19,27,28

The promises of Jesus to his disciples give us clues in our search for peace, for faith, for the nature of the relationship we continue to have with our child who has died.

Someone has said that children who have died are with us in a constant way that living children can never be. We also know the pain of the reverse of that statement, that the child who is dead cannot be with us in ways we yearn for, to put our arms around and hold close. But in our hearts, after a while, we come to know the truth of the child's presence, close as our own skin, integral to our life as the beating of our heart. It is not what we would have wished, but it is a gift, a gracious presence, as are the memories we have, the reflections of the child's personality we may discover in ourselves now, and in others who are close.

Is there more? Is it all memory and unfolding from the past? Is it possible to be in touch with the dead? "Do you hear from her?" a young woman asked when I told her of my sorrow. I didn't know what to say. "Not as I'd like to. Maybe. I'm not sure. I sometimes have a strong sense of her."

Stories of communicating with the dead go all the way from thoughts of a loved one staying persistently in our minds to people who have reported experiences of seeing, hearing, and speaking with the spirits of those they love. We are so eager. We would like to believe, but we do not want to be duped or misled.

We do not understand the work of the Spirit among the living—why two people's thoughts may turn simultaneously to one another though they are a thousand miles apart, how some people seem to have a sense of what is about to happen, how the energy of prayer surrounds us. How did the Holy Spirit descend on the believers at Pentecost? What happened to Paul on the Damascus Road? How did the two disciples see Jesus on the road to Emmaus?

These are mysteries, the mysteries of God. We need to be wary of our own susceptibility to wishful thinking. We may do equal disservice to the truth by being too skeptical.

Whose need is it, and what do we need? Once I asked a woman I trusted and who has had many experiences of spiritual presence in her own life, "Do you think we have a responsibility to try to be in touch with the dead?" (I was still wondering whether for me to go on about my life was to abandon my daughter. What if she was looking for me and I wasn't paying attention?) The woman said, "Don't worry about it. It's bad to go around with your head in that. If you need it, you'll get it." It helped me to relinquish my anxiety, to recognize it was my need I was expressing, and to trust the processes of life and of God to give me what I need.

A New Heaven and a New Earth

"The resurrection takes on meaning for us when we begin to people heaven with our loves," a friend wrote us after the death of our daughter. Surely our investment in the other side of death is greater than it was, for a part of our heart's home is there uniquely in our child. If we are stronger now in our faith, if we feel that at a deep level of our being that question is answered, then we are freer to savor the life we have with more abandon, more joy. For it is the Christian claim that we *can* "have our cake and eat it, too," that beyond this life in which we take delight and beyond the loves we experience here are life and love unfathomably greater.

In *Living and Dying*, Lifton and Olson have suggested, "The survivor is one for whom having known the end makes possible a new beginning." One does not survive intact. One comes through and is a different person, a new person. The Christian story of death and rebirth is a promise that on the other side of death are reunion and light and growth and love. It is also a paradigm of grief and rebirth in the life that we have here and now. It is different now, it is not the same. It is not even the same with one major exception. It is all different. We have experienced a death of a part of ourselves in the death of our child. But we are here. We are not destroyed. We are, in fact, made strong. We are reborn, and lo—all things are become new.

"The highest tribute to the dead," wrote Wilder, "is not grief but gratitude." And not gratitude for them alone, but for all the gifts of God, all grace, all wonders, all reopening of the stunned pores of love so we can be vulnerable again, all joy in the evenings and mornings of our lives, and all expectation that we can meet life's recurring crises. For look what we have been through already! Like Daniel, we have been in the fire, yet we are not consumed.

In the Old Testament are the words, "I have set before you this day life and . . . death. . . . Therefore choose life" (Deut. 30:15,19). It is a choice we can make—daily, hourly, a minute or a day at a time— leaning into our lives, trusting that the future, as the past, is with God, that the secrets of the future will bring their own message to us in their own time, and that at the moment of our death the child who has left us will be there, to welcome us home.

Organizations

Below is a list of organizations (some with chapters in many cities) which address themselves to the needs of bereaved parents and families who have experienced the death of a child.

Candlelighters Childhood Cancer Foundation, 7910 Woodmont Ave., Suite 460, Bethesda, MD 20814; Tel. 800/366-2223. An organization for parents whose children are on or off treatment for cancer or those who have lost a child to cancer.

Compassionate Friends, P.O. Box 3696, Oak Brook, IL 60522-3696; Tel. 708/990-0010. A self-help organization for parents and siblings who have experienced the death of a child.

Parents of Murdered Children, 108 East 8th St., B-41, Cincinnati, OH 45202; Tel. 513/721-5683. An organization of parents and families who have experienced the death of a child through homicide. Also provides information about the criminal justice system.

Sudden Infant Death Syndrome (SIDS) Alliance, 10500 Little Patuxent Parkway, Suite 420, Columbia, MD

21044; Tel. 800/221-7437. An organization to help families who have lost a child through sudden, unexplained death, often called crib death.

Books

Many books on grief are available. This short list is limited to those on the death of children.

The Bereaved Parent by Harriet Sarnoff Schiff (New York: Penguin Books, 1978). Offers step-by-step analysis and counsel by a woman whose son died after illness.

Five Cries of Grief by Merton P. Strommer and A. Irene Strommer (New York: HarperCollins, 1993). How two parents coped with the tragic death by lightning of a twenty-five-year-old son.

Guests of My Life by Elizabeth Watson (Burnsville, N. C.: Celo Press, 1979). A woman whose daughter died in an accident tells how she was helped by the poetry and prose of six great writers.

Helping Children Grieve by Theresa Huntley (Minneapolis: Augsburg, 1991). Patterns of grieving and ways of helping other children in the family. Includes extensive bibliography for further reading.

Hour of Gold, Hour of Lead by Anne Morrow Lindbergh (New York: New American Library, 1974). A journal including reflections on grief and recovery after the

kidnap and murder of her infant son.

On Children and Death by Elisabeth Kubler-Ross (New York: Macmillan, 1983). The noted psychiatrist offers loving and practical help from her experience working with dying children and bereavement.

When Bad Things Happen to Good People by Harold Kushner (New York: Shocken Books, 1981). A rabbi whose son dies after a disfiguring illness confronts the problems of suffering and grief